To my husband John and our two blessings from God,
Skylar & Asher, who encourage, challenge, and inspire
me to live out my faith each and every day.

Table of Contents

A note from the Author

Hello, beautiful!! I'm SO glad you're here! This prayer journal came about at a pretty monumental time in my life. 2018 was a tough year for me—filled with trials and debilitating illnesses. These matters prevented me from doing things I was passionate about, and threw me into a tailspin of fear, doubt, and insecurity. I lost friendships, racked up extensive medical bills, and found myself desperate to understand why all of this was happening to me. Throughout the year, I kept asking God why He was allowing this pain in my life. What good could possibly come from something so hard and difficult? What was He trying to teach me through all of this?

The harder things got, the more I found myself clinging to God and His promises, crying out for healing, restoration, and understanding. I have never had more appreciation for my family and close friends after the things I went through this year. As I was healing over the summer, I read several powerful books, including one about the many ways that God speaks to us, and another about the importance of prayer and its powerful impact. Little did I know then, that God had been paving the way for this little prayer journal project all along. When I was asked to write a prayer journal, I was hesitant at first, feeling unequipped and unqualified for the job. However, through all of this, I've learned that if God calls you to it, He will qualify you for it—no resumé needed! Here I am today writing this, significantly healthier than I was, able to look back, and more grateful than ever for my life, and the ways that God continues to bless it in spite of the storms and mistakes that I make on a daily basis.

God promises to be with us throughout this journey called life, through the mountains and valleys, the highs and the lows. My hope and prayer is that this journal will strengthen your faith and your walk with God, no matter what season of life you find yourself in. God is always at work and promises to work all things out for the good of those who love Him! I hope that you will record your thoughts, prayers, and deepest desires, and that you will be able to look back and see the incredible ways that God has moved with you over the year. Thank you for allowing me to be a small part of your walk with our almighty God and Savior! May God bless you beyond measure!

About this Journal

Your prayer journal consists of four different sections:

Scripture

Reflect

Journal

Answered Prayers:

The next few pages will explain these areas in detail, so that you can get the most out of using your journal and connecting with God!

Scripture

Each week (52 total) features a new Bible verse to reflect and meditate on throughout your week, giving you time to memorize the verse and ingrain it into your heart and mind.

JAMES 1:19

My dear brothers and sisters, take note of this: Everyone should be *quick to listen, slow to speak* and *slow to become angry.*

Reflect

LOVE & INNER BEAUTY

Have you ever formed (and perhaps even shared!) an opinion about something, only to change your stance once you learned more about the subject? Have you ever lost your temper, or jumped to a conclusion? How did these experiences make you feel? God calls us to listen thoughtfully, to be slow to speak, and to keep our tempers under control. Are any of these things difficult for you? Why do you think this is? Have you shared your heart with God?

Each week also includes a "Reflect" page, with thoughts and questions prompted by the weekly Scripture, and space for you to record your thoughts and responses. You may use this as an ongoing weekly reflection or fill the space in a single day! Remember: this journal is flexible for what works best with your schedule—and your walk with God.

Journal

What week is it? Record the date and watch how God moves with you throughout the year!

In what areas of your life do you desire growth? Share your thoughts and ask God to teach you!

What are you thankful for this week? Let God know how grateful you are for His blessings in your life.

What are some areas of your life that you desire God's guidance in? Share your thoughts with Him! He's always listening!

♡LORD♡
thank you

WEEK OF:

teach me

guide me

PSALM 145:8

The Lord is gracious and compassionate, slow to anger and rich in love.

things on my heart:

highlights

prayer requests

Each week includes a special verse that is specifically about prayer. (This is different from the weekly reflection verse.)

What is on your heart this week? Write down whatever is tugging at your heart and occupying your thoughts.

Record your prayers. Again, you can write all in one sitting, or record your prayers throughout the week.

Life is fast-paced and non-stop at times. Take time to write down the special, precious things that happen during your day-to-day each week!

Answered Prayers

Answered Prayers

PRAYER REQUEST	PRAYER DATE	DATE ANSWERED

Record your prayer requests in the space provided.

Also, record the date that you FIRST began praying this particular request.

Record the date that the prayer was answered. Watch how God moves with you and answers your prayers this year! Trust in His timing and how much He loves you!

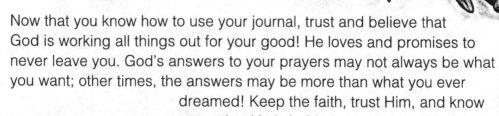

Now that you know how to use your journal, trust and believe that God is working all things out for your good! He loves and promises to never leave you. God's answers to your prayers may not always be what you want; other times, the answers may be more than what you ever dreamed! Keep the faith, trust Him, and know that He is behind, present, and before you in all things!

JAMES 1:19

My dear brothers and sisters, take note of this: Everyone should be *quick to listen, slow to speak* and *slow to become angry.*

Reflect

Much has been said about the power of gratitude: those
who pause to "count their blessings" are happier, more joyful people.

For whom and what are you thankful? How has God blessed your life?
How are you a blessing in the lives of others?

_____
_____
_____
_____
_____
_____
_____
_____
_____
_____
_____

_____
_____
_____
_____
_____
_____
_____
_____

1 THESSALONIANS 5:16-18

Rejoice always, pray continually, give thanks in all circumstances; for this is God's will for you in Christ Jesus.

things on my heart:

_____
_____
_____
_____
_____
_____
_____

highlights

_____
_____
_____
_____
_____
_____
_____

prayer requests

_____
_____
_____
_____
_____
_____

ISAIAH 43:2

When you pass
through the waters,
I will be with you;
and when you pass through
the rivers, they will not
sweep over you. When you
walk through the fire, you will
not be burned; the flames
will not set you ablaze.

REFLECT

ADVERSITY & TRIALS

God promises to never leave you. He is with you wherever you go,
and in whatever circumstance you find yourself in.

Think about a difficult time during your life. Did you feel God's presence? Are you able to look back and recognize that God was with you during that time? What comfort can you draw from this knowledge now? How might this knowledge and awareness sustain you as you encounter challenging times in the future?

_____

_____

_____

_____

_____

_____

_____

_____

_____

_____

_____

_____

_____

_____

_____

_____

_____

_____

_____

_____

LORD, thank you

teach me

guide me

PSALM 18:6

In my distress I called to the Lord; I cried to my God for help. From his temple he heard my voice; my cry came before him, into his ears.

_____
_____
_____
_____
_____
_____
_____

highlights

_____
_____
_____
_____
_____
_____

_____
_____
_____
_____
_____
_____

PSALM 139:13-14

For you created my inmost
being; you knit me together
in my mother's womb.

*I praise you because
I am fearfully and
wonderfully made;*

your works are wonderful,
I know that full well.

AWE & SOVEREIGNTY

You are a one-of-a-kind, beautiful soul with unique talents, gifts, and abilities in a body that is exclusively yours. With over seven billion people in this world and only one you, God must have had some pretty big plans for you when He created you!

Do you believe that you are His handiwork, and that you are fearfully and wonderfully made? List your characteristics and attributes that you are grateful for. What do you cherish about yourself? Are there any ways that you wish you were different? How can God use ALL of you to accomplish His will for your life?

_____

_____

_____

_____

_____

_____

_____

_____

_____

_____

_____

_____

_____

_____

_____

_____

_____

_____

_____

_____

_____

LORD, thank you

teach me

_____
_____
_____
_____
_____
_____
_____
_____
_____
_____
_____

guide me

_____
_____
_____
_____
_____
_____
_____
_____
_____

JOHN 15:16

You did not choose me, but I chose you and appointed you so that you might go and bear fruit—fruit that will last—and so that whatever you ask in my name the Father will give you.

things on my heart:

_____
_____
_____
_____
_____
_____

highlights

_____
_____
_____
_____
_____
_____

prayer requests

_____
_____
_____
_____
_____
_____

GENESIS 28:15

I am with you
and will watch over you
wherever you go, and I will
bring you back to this land.

I will not leave you
until I have done
what I have
promised you.

STRENGTH THROUGH FAITH

What an awesome peace you can have knowing that God promises to be with you wherever you go! He has a special plan for your life and won't ever leave you. No matter the season of life you're in, the hardships you're facing, or the uncertainty you're handling, God is with you.

List your worries and cares, and your hopes and joys. Pause to lift these thoughts to God in prayer, trusting that God will always meet your needs and never leave you.

_____
_____
_____
_____
_____
_____
_____
_____
_____
_____
_____
_____
_____
_____
_____
_____
_____
_____
_____
_____

LORD,
thank you

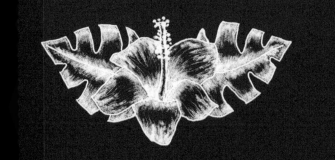

teach me

_____
_____
_____
_____
_____
_____
_____
_____
_____

guide me

_____
_____
_____
_____
_____
_____
_____
_____

1 TIMOTHY 2:1-2

I urge, then, first of all, that petitions, prayers, intercession and thanksgiving be made for all people—for kings and all those in authority, that we may live peaceful and quiet lives in all godliness and holiness.

things on my heart:

_____
_____
_____
_____
_____
_____

highlights

_____
_____
_____
_____
_____
_____

prayer requests

_____
_____
_____
_____
_____
_____
_____

DEUTERONOMY 31:8

The Lord himself goes
before you and will
be with you;

*he will never
leave you nor
forsake you.*

Do not be afraid; do
not be discouraged.

REFLECT

FEAR

Life is often unpredictable. You might find yourself in a place you never imagined you'd be in at this point. You may find yourself discouraged about that job you didn't get, the spouse you haven't found yet, the disappointment of your current marriage, or even the fear of a recent diagnosis of you or a loved one. You can find refuge in Christ knowing that He goes behind, with, and before you, and will never leave you. He's walking your journey right along with you and knew about the circumstances you would find yourself in long before they ever came or will come to be.

What is weighing on your heart right now? Give it to God. He's here. He's listening, and He's already ahead of you watching over every step you take.

_____

_____

_____

_____

_____

_____

_____

_____

_____

_____

_____

_____

_____

_____

_____

_____

_____

_____

_____

_____

LORD, thank you

teach me

guide me

ROMANS 12:12

Be joyful in hope, patient in affliction, faithful in prayer.

things on my heart:

_____
_____
_____
_____
_____
_____
_____

highlights

_____
_____
_____
_____
_____
_____

prayer requests

_____
_____
_____
_____
_____
_____

1 JOHN 1:9

If we confess our sins,
he is faithful
and just
and will forgive us
our sins and
purify us from all
unrighteousness.

GRACE & FORGIVENESS

God is merciful and forgiving—such a simple statement with such a huge meaning. As humans, we lack the capacity to fully understand just how majestic and glorious He is, and yet, here we are, these tiny specs in an enormous universe, that He created and LOVES so very much! He desires your heart—all of it. Whatever sin(s) you've committed, or whatever guilt you are facing as a result of that sin, bring it first and foremost to God. For ALL have sinned—that includes a lot of people, yet God promises to forgive and purify us from our unrighteous behavior if we confess our sins to Him.

Are there any areas in your life weighing heavy on your heart as a result of sinful decisions? Have you taken this to God and asked for His forgiveness? Do you believe that God has forgiven you?

Write your thoughts below.

_____

_____

_____

_____

_____

_____

_____

_____

_____

_____

_____

_____

_____

_____

_____

_____

_____

LORD, thank you

teach me

_____
_____
_____
_____
_____
_____
_____
_____
_____
_____
_____
_____
_____
_____
_____

guide me

_____
_____
_____
_____
_____
_____
_____
_____
_____

JAMES 5:16

Therefore confess your sins to each other and pray for each other so that you may be healed. The prayer of a righteous person is powerful and effective.

things on my heart:

_____
_____
_____
_____
_____
_____
_____

_____
_____
_____
_____
_____
_____

_____
_____
_____
_____
_____
_____

1 PETER 3:3-4

Your beauty should not come
from outward adornment, such as
elaborate hairstyles and the wearing
of gold jewelry or fine clothes. Rather,
it should be that of your inner self,

*the unfading
beauty of a gentle
and quiet spirit,*

which is of great worth in God's sight.

REFLECT

LOVE & INNER BEAUTY

We live in a world where there is so much pressure to look a certain way, dress to impress, and avoid ever-showing signs of aging. It's no wonder the cosmetic, fashion, and plastic surgery industries are such big money makers in today's society! There is nothing wrong with wanting to look good on the outside. In fact, some of us feel our absolute best on the inside when we feel outwardly beautiful. However, God values what's going on inside of you most! He looks at your heart. He desires for you to have a gentle and quiet spirit, to be quick to love and slow to anger.

Do you feel pressure in today's society to look a certain way? Do you put more emphasis on your outward appearance, or on your inward beauty? What are some ways that you can focus more on God's desires for your inner self?

_____

_____

_____

_____

_____

_____

_____

_____

_____

_____

_____

_____

_____

_____

_____

_____

LORD, thank you

teach me

guide me

2 CHRONICLES 7:14

If my people, who are called by my name, will humble themselves and pray and seek my face and turn from their wicked ways, then I will hear from heaven, and I will forgive their sin and will heal their land.

things on my heart:

_____
_____
_____
_____
_____
_____
_____

highlights

_____
_____
_____
_____
_____
_____
_____

prayer requests

_____
_____
_____
_____
_____
_____
_____

EPHESIANS 2:10

For we are God's handiwork,

created in Christ Jesus
to do good works,

which God prepared in
advance for us to do.

PROVISION & FAITHFULNESS

Have you ever stopped to consider that you were created by God—the almighty creator of the entire universe?! He is the ultimate artist, and you are His beautiful masterpiece, gifted with unique abilities and talents.

What "good works" do you feel God has called you to do?
What are your God-given gifts, talents, and desires?
How can you align your gifts and God's calling in a way that blesses others?

_____
_____
_____
_____
_____
_____
_____
_____
_____
_____
_____
_____
_____
_____
_____
_____
_____
_____
_____

LORD, thank you

WEEK OF:

teach me

guide me

JOHN 14:13

And I will do whatever you ask in my name, so that the
Father may be glorified in the Son.

things on my heart:

_____
_____
_____
_____
_____
_____
_____

highlights

_____
_____
_____
_____
_____

prayer requests

_____
_____
_____
_____
_____
_____

GALATIANS 6:2

Carry each other's burdens, and in this way you will fulfill the law of Christ.

ADVERSITY & TRIALS

God has placed you exactly where you are right in this moment. The people in your circle (including your friends, co-workers, neighbors), the family you have, and the circumstances you find yourself in are all part of God's plan for your life!

Who are the people in your life whom you rely on to help you carry your burdens? Who relies on you? In what way? How have you experienced God's grace through sharing your burdens and supporting others in their times of struggle?

_____
_____
_____
_____
_____
_____
_____
_____
_____
_____
_____
_____
_____
_____
_____
_____
_____
_____
_____
_____

LORD, thank you

teach me

_____
_____
_____
_____
_____
_____
_____
_____
_____
_____
_____

guide me

_____
_____
_____
_____
_____
_____
_____
_____
_____

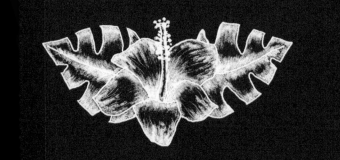

PSALM 34:17

The righteous cry out, and the Lord hears them; he delivers them from all their troubles.

things on my heart:

_____
_____
_____
_____
_____
_____
_____
_____

highlights

_____
_____
_____
_____
_____
_____
_____

prayer requests

_____
_____
_____
_____
_____
_____
_____

PSALM 147:3

He *heals* the
brokenhearted
and *binds up*
their wounds.

REFLECT

GOD'S LOVE

God's love is a balm to heartbreak, just as time heals a wound of the flesh. You can have assurance knowing that God is your ultimate healer and He loves you so much! He desires your heart and a loving, intimate relationship with you, and He will never forsake you.

Have you ever suffered a broken heart, or another painful life experience? Did you go to God during that time? How did you encounter God's comfort and love? How does this verse encourage you going forward?

_____

_____

_____

_____

_____

_____

_____

_____

_____

_____

_____

_____

_____

_____

_____

_____

_____

_____

_____

LORD, thank you

teach me

guide me

PSALM 145:18-19

The Lord is near to all who call on him, to all who call on him in truth. He fulfills the desires of those who fear him; he hears their cry and saves them.

things on my heart:

_____
_____
_____
_____
_____
_____
_____

highlights

_____
_____
_____
_____
_____
_____
_____
_____

prayer requests

_____
_____
_____
_____
_____
_____
_____

EPHESIANS 3:20-21

Now to him who is able
to do immeasurably more
than all we ask or imagine,
according to his power
that is at work within us,

*to him be glory
in the church and
in Christ Jesus*

throughout all generations,
for ever and ever! Amen.

AWE & SOVEREIGNTY

Are you a dreamer? Do you have goals and aspirations that you want to accomplish in your lifetime? Do you realize that the God of the universe who dwells within you can accomplish more through you than you could ever ask or imagine for yourself?! He can use you in ways you never thought possible. Those dreams and goals that you have—hold on to them! You never know how God will use your heart's desires and goals to accomplish His perfect purpose for your life. Keep dreaming and keep relying on Him and His perfect timing, and know that you have those desires for a reason!

Write about the dreams and goals you have for your life. Do you trust that God has placed you exactly where you are for His perfect purpose? Do you share your hopes and dreams with God?

_____

_____

_____

_____

_____

_____

_____

_____

_____

_____

_____

_____

_____

_____

_____

_____

_____

LORD, thank you

teach me

guide me

1 JOHN 5:14

This is the confidence we have in approaching God: that if we ask anything according to his will, he hears us.

things on my heart:

_____
_____
_____
_____
_____
_____
_____

highlights

_____
_____
_____
_____
_____

prayer requests

_____
_____
_____
_____
_____

67

PSALM 46:5

God is within her,
she will not fall:
God will help
her at the break
of day.

REFLECT

STRENGTH THROUGH FAITH

How might you welcome each new day with intention, hope, and joy?
Reflect on how God dwells within you and the encouragement that His promises bring.
How does this knowledge influence how you go about your day-to-day activities?

LORD, thank you

WEEK OF:

teach me

guide me

PSALM 5:3

In the morning, Lord, you hear my voice; in the morning I lay my requests before you and wait expectantly.

things on my heart:

_____
_____
_____
_____
_____
_____
_____

highlights

_____
_____
_____
_____
_____
_____

prayer requests

_____
_____
_____
_____
_____
_____
_____

PHILIPPIANS 4:6-7

Do not be anxious about anything, but in every situation, by prayer and petition, with thanksgiving, present your requests to God. And the *peace of God,* which transcends all understanding, will guard your hearts and your minds in Christ Jesus.

FER

We live in a fallen world, where the enemy lurks and heartbreaking news seems to be the norm. It's no wonder that anxiety and fear are so prevalent today. God wants you to share your worries with Him, and in turn His peace will guard your heart and mind in Christ Jesus!

Do you ever find yourself crippled by anxieties and worries? How do you cope with them? Is your first instinct to bring these worries to God? Take this opportunity to list the things that weigh heavy on your heart. Reflect on how you can present these "with thanksgiving" to God.

LORD, thank you

teach me

guide me

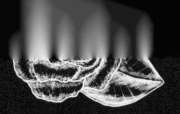

things on my heart:

_____
_____
_____
_____
_____
_____

highlights

_____
_____
_____
_____
_____

prayer requests

_____
_____
_____
_____
_____
_____

MICAH 6:8

He has shown you, O mortal, what is good. And what does the Lord require of you? To *act justly and to love mercy and to walk humbly* with your God.

LOVE & INNER BEAUTY

It's funny how we sometimes act entitled: "I accomplished X, Y, Z, so I deserve ____." Or, "You caused me pain or heartache, so you deserve ____". It's easy to get caught-up in feeling "holi-er-than-thou" and to miss the bigger picture.

God calls us to act justly and to love mercy. These qualities seem to oppose each other: justice = equality and fair treatment, while mercy = forgiveness and compassion. At first glance, these seem to conflict, but they actually work harmoniously together, just as Christ models for us in Scripture when He mercifully died on the cross for our sins. To top it off, we are called to walk humbly with God! God is so much bigger than our egos and our self-righteousness. He desires our hearts to earnestly follow Him and His will for our lives!

Do you struggle in any of these areas? What are some ways that you can demonstrate the qualities that God desires of you to those around you?

_____
_____
_____
_____
_____
_____
_____
_____
_____
_____
_____
_____
_____

LORD, thank you

WEEK OF: _____

teach me

_____
_____
_____
_____
_____
_____
_____
_____
_____
_____

guide me

_____
_____
_____
_____
_____
_____
_____
_____

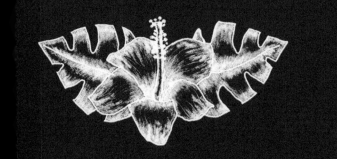

ROMANS 8:26

In the same way, the Spirit helps us in our weakness. We do not know what we ought to pray for, but the Spirit himself intercedes for us through wordless groans.

things on my heart:

_____
_____
_____
_____
_____
_____

highlights

prayer requests

_____
_____
_____
_____
_____
_____

JAMES 1:5

If any of you
lacks wisdom, you
should ask God,
*who gives
generously to all*
without finding fault,
and it will be
given to you.

REFLECT

PROVISION & FAITHFULNESS

Life is full of unpredictable moments, including some that you may feel too inexperienced to handle. You might feel that there is someone else who would deal better with a situation that God has placed in your life. On the contrary, God desires for you to go straight to Him, especially when you doubt your own abilities! He will give you the wisdom and understanding to handle those moments the best way possible.

What do you do when you are faced with difficulty or are unsure about something?
Write about an experience God brought you through that you didn't know how to handle at first.

_____
_____
_____
_____
_____
_____
_____
_____
_____
_____
_____
_____
_____
_____
_____
_____
_____
_____
_____
_____

LORD, thank you

WEEK OF:

teach me

_____
_____
_____
_____
_____
_____
_____
_____

guide me

_____
_____
_____
_____
_____
_____
_____
_____

1 JOHN 3:21-22

Dear friends, if our hearts do not condemn us, we have confidence before God and receive from him anything we ask, because we keep his commands and do what pleases him.

things on my heart:

highlights

prayer requests

1 KINGS 19:11-13

The Lord said, "Go out and stand on the mountain in the presence of the Lord, for the Lord is about to pass by."

Then a great and powerful wind tore the mountains apart and shattered the rocks before the Lord, but the Lord was not in the wind. After the wind there was an earthquake, but the Lord was not in the earthquake. After the earthquake came a fire, but the Lord was not in the fire. And after the fire came

a gentle whisper.

When Elijah heard it, he pulled his cloak over his face and went out and stood at the mouth of the cave.

GOD'S LOVE

Have you ever pondered the significance of this scripture? Elijah is hiding in a cave, fearing for his life when the Lord tells Him he wants him to go out and stand on the mountain in the presence of the Lord, for He is about to pass by. Elijah waits as a powerful wind, an earthquake, and fire appear, one after the other. Then, there's a gentle whisper. At hearing this, Elijah gets up and goes out, knowing it's the Lord.

Sometimes, we get so wrapped up in our day-to-day busy lives that we forget to pause, be still, and listen for God's voice speaking to us. That still, small voice, that whisper—it's intimate. You can't whisper to someone who's across the room. They have to be near to hear. This speaks volumes about who God is. He's close by—near enough that He can speak to you in a gentle whisper!

Have you ever had an experience in which you just knew that God was speaking to you? What was this like for you? Do you sometimes struggle to make time to be still and listen to what He has to say? What are ways that you can become a better listener? Write your thoughts below.

_____

_____

_____

_____

_____

_____

_____

_____

_____

_____

_____

_____

_____

LORD, thank you

teach me

guide me

JEREMIAH 29:12

Then you will call on me and come and
pray to me, and I will listen to you.

things on my heart:

_____
_____
_____
_____
_____
_____
_____

highlights

_____
_____
_____
_____
_____
_____

prayer requests

_____
_____
_____
_____
_____
_____

ROMANS 5:3-5

Not only so, but we also *glory in our sufferings,* because we know that suffering produces perseverance; perseverance, character; and character, hope. And hope does not put us to shame, because *God's love has been poured out into our hearts* through the Holy Spirit, who has been given to us.

REFLECT

ADVERSITY & TRIALS

Christianity and suffering are a package deal. While difficult, trials and hard times can result in enormous positives, both for yourself and for others. Life's difficulties can actually serve to draw you closer to God, and other beautiful outcomes! When you feel like your world is crumbling around you, know that God is right there walking the journey alongside you. He is looking forward to hearing from you! God uses these experiences to shape your heart and character, and to provide hope and support to others who may someday face a similar situation.

Are you going through a trying time or suffering now? Have you ever gone through an experience that gave someone else hope after they watched you walk through it? Write about a trial you faced that changed you and your perspective.

_____

_____

_____

_____

_____

_____

_____

_____

_____

_____

_____

_____

_____

_____

_____

_____

JAMES 5:13

Is anyone among you in trouble?
Let them pray. Is anyone happy?
Let them sing songs of praise.

things on my heart:

highlights

prayer requests

91

PROVERBS 19:21

Many are the
plans in a person's
heart, but
*it is the Lord's
purpose
that prevails.*

AWE & SOVEREIGNTY

Have confidence and know that God can (and will!) use any situation or circumstance in your life for His good and perfect purpose. That is so encouraging! Your choices—both good and bad—God can use ALL of them for His purpose.

How many times have you gone down a path or made plans for your life, only to encounter unexpected turns along the way? Where did these turns lead? Did they bring you closer to God or distance you from Him? Reflect and write about your experience(s).

And if we know that he hears us—whatever we ask—we know
that we have what we asked of him.

_____
_____
_____
_____
_____
_____

_____
_____
_____
_____
_____
_____
_____

_____
_____
_____
_____
_____
_____
_____

HEBREWS 11:6

And without faith it is impossible to please God,

because anyone who comes to him must believe that he exists and that he rewards those who earnestly seek him.

STRENGTH THROUGH FAITH

Have you ever wrestled with doubt? For most people, doubt can creep in, oftentimes when you're facing something really difficult, or when you're unsure of a decision. You may wonder why God would allow this or that to happen. You may even wonder if He's really there when you are in so much pain, or if He actually hears your prayers when you don't feel that you can hear anything back from Him. You may feel called to do something but wonder if it's truly the right thing for you to do.

As believers, it's normal to have doubts—we are human after all. However, this is where faith steps in. Faith is having confidence in what we hope for and is the evidence of things we don't see (Hebrews 11:1). Look around you. Consider this: if you can look at a wristwatch and know without a doubt that it was created by someone, how much more can you look at the world around you—in all of its beauty and complexity—and know with certainty that our master creator is behind it all?

Have you ever struggled with your faith in God? How did you overcome your doubts?
Did you seek Him through uncertain times? Write about these experiences below.

_____

_____

_____

_____

_____

_____

_____

_____

_____

_____

_____

_____

_____

LORD,
thank you

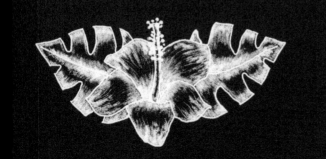

teach me

guide me

JAMES 1:6

But when you ask, you must believe and not doubt,
because the one who doubts is like a wave of the sea,
blown and tossed by the wind.

things on my heart:

_____
_____
_____
_____
_____
_____

highlights

_____
_____
_____
_____
_____
_____

prayer requests

_____
_____
_____
_____
_____
_____
_____

EPHESIANS 4:32

Be *kind and compassionate* to one another, *forgiving* each other, just as in Christ God forgave you.

REFLECT

GRACE & FORGIVENESS

Forgiveness. It can be so difficult at times, can't it? How dare that person cut me off while driving? How dare my spouse speak to me that way? How dare my kids leave this mess for me to clean up? How dare all of them!

Well, not so fast. Scripture tells us that we are all sinners, and that we ALL fall short of God's glory. Forgiveness is at the root of who God is, and why He sent His son Jesus Christ to die on the cross for us! We don't deserve God's forgiveness or mercy, but He freely gives it, allowing us to have a relationship with Him. Now that is love!

Are you someone who holds grudges, or do you find it easy to forgive others?
How do you handle the challenge of forgiving someone, especially when you don't want to?

_____
_____
_____
_____
_____
_____
_____
_____
_____
_____
_____
_____
_____
_____
_____
_____
_____

LORD, thank you

teach me

guide me

LUKE 6:27-28

But to you who are listening I say: Love your enemies, do good to those who hate you, bless those who curse you, pray for those who mistreat you.

things on my heart

highlights

prayer requests

PROVERBS 4:23

Above all else,
*guard your
heart,*
for everything
you do flows
from it.

LOVE & INNER BEAUTY

The human heart is an incredible organ. It is tied to our physical well-being, but is also tied to our spiritual health. From a spiritual perspective, our desires, thoughts, feelings, emotions, and actions reflect what is going on at the core of our hearts. In order to protect it best, God desires us to be in tune with Him and His word.

Has your spiritual heart health ever been compromised? How did you cope with it? What did you do in order to heal and to get back in tune with God's desires for you?

_____

_____

_____

_____

_____

_____

_____

_____

_____

_____

_____

_____

_____

_____

_____

_____

_____

_____

LORD, thank you

teach me

guide me

MATTHEW 6:6

But when you pray, go into your room, close the door and pray to your Father, who is unseen. Then your Father, who sees what is done in secret, will reward you.

things on my heart:

_____
_____
_____
_____
_____

_____
_____
_____
_____
_____
_____
_____

_____
_____
_____
_____
_____
_____
_____

HEBREWS 13:5

Keep your lives free from
the love of money and
*be content with
what you have,*
because God has said,
"Never will I leave you;
never will I forsake you."

REFLECT

PROVISION & FAITHFULNESS

As a society, we are conditioned to want more and better: nicer clothes, fancier cars, bigger houses. Modern advertising feeds the notion that we should constantly "upgrade."

Are you a person who is content with what you have, or do you seek "more?" In what ways has God provided for you? Do you trust that God will always provide for your needs?

1 PETER 4:7

The end of all things is near. Therefore be
alert and of sober mind so that you may pray.

things on my heart:

_____
_____
_____
_____
_____
_____

highlights

_____
_____
_____
_____
_____
_____

prayer requests

_____
_____
_____
_____
_____

JAMES 1:2-4

Consider it pure joy, my brothers and sisters, whenever you face trials of many kinds, because you know that the

testing of your faith produces perseverance.

Let perseverance finish its work so that you may be mature and complete, not lacking anything.

ADVERSITY & TRIALS

Trial, hardship, challenge, adversity, tough times—it is difficult to read these words with positive associations. However, these are the very things that help you grow as a believer. They require you to persevere, which in turn grows confidence and maturity—and even produces joy! Hard times often end up steering the people enduring them toward God, which in turn encourages growth in their relationship with Him. God may even use your life experiences to benefit someone else one day!

What hardships have you overcome in the past? What trials do you currently face? How have these experiences shaped you as a person? Have they tested you? How have they strengthened your faith?

PSALM 34:15

The eyes of the Lord are on the righteous,
and his ears are attentive to their cry.

things on my heart:

_____
_____
_____
_____
_____
_____
_____
_____

highlights

_____
_____
_____
_____
_____
_____
_____

prayer requests

_____
_____
_____
_____
_____
_____
_____

MATTHEW 5:14-16

You are the light of the world.

A town built on a hill cannot be hidden. Neither do people light a lamp and put it under a bowl. Instead they put it on its stand, and it gives light to everyone in the house. In the same way,

let your light shine

before others, that they may see your good deeds and glorify your Father in heaven.

Reflect

GOD'S LOVE

In the same way that a lamp lights up a room, believers are called to let their light shine. That light is the Holy Spirit living within you. When you became saved, you were a new creation, filled with the Holy Spirit—you are the light of the world! As a Christian, you have a calling. People are watching you. Your actions, words, deeds, and how you love others (while perhaps imperfect—you are human!), should reflect the inner workings of your salvation and God's love. There is a hope inside of you that others are so desperately searching for, and by shining your light for others to see, you can gently point people toward God!

What are some ways that you can let your light shine to others? Has anyone ever told you that they noticed something different about you, about how you live your life?
What does this verse mean to you?

_____
_____
_____
_____
_____
_____
_____
_____
_____
_____
_____
_____
_____
_____
_____

teach me

guide me

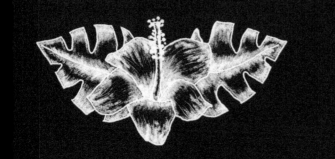

PROVERBS 15:29

The Lord is far from the wicked, but he hears the prayer of the righteous.

things on my heart:

_____
_____
_____
_____
_____
_____

highlights

_____
_____
_____
_____
_____

prayer requests

_____
_____
_____
_____
_____

GALATIANS 6:9

Let us not
become weary
in doing good,
for at the proper
time we will
reap a harvest
if we do
not give up.

REFLECT

AWE & SOVEREIGNTY

It's a fact: modern life can all-too-often be hectic and overwhelming, but you can rest assured that God knows what you are going through and He's right there with you through it all. He wants you to keep pressing on, doing good, and loving others, for in His good and perfect timing, you will see the fruits of those actions and behaviors!

Do you find it challenging to juggle the demands of your time? Do you trust that God has placed you exactly where you are in your life for His good and perfect purpose for you? Reflect on your challenges and how God may be using these for His greater purpose.

_____
_____
_____
_____
_____
_____
_____
_____
_____
_____
_____
_____
_____
_____
_____
_____
_____
_____
_____
_____

LORD, thank you

teach me

_____
_____
_____
_____
_____
_____
_____
_____
_____
_____

guide me

_____
_____
_____
_____
_____
_____
_____
_____
_____

_____
_____
_____
_____
_____
_____
_____
_____
_____
_____
_____
_____
_____
_____
_____
_____
_____
_____
_____
_____
_____
_____
_____
_____
_____
_____
_____

things on my heart:

_____
_____
_____
_____
_____
_____

highlights

_____
_____
_____
_____
_____
_____

prayer requests

_____
_____
_____
_____
_____
_____

PSALM 121:2

My help comes from the Lord, the Maker of heaven and earth.

STRENGTH THROUGH FAITH

God is your ultimate helper! He is always there for you, in both good times and bad.

What is your first inclination when you are faced with adversity? Do you turn to worldly remedies, or do you bring your troubles to God first? What challenges are you facing in your life right now? Have you given them to God, trusting that He hears you and knows what you need? Write about your challenges below and lay your cares before God.

LORD, thank you

teach me

guide me

PSALM 17:6

I call on you, my God, for you will answer me;
turn your ear to me and hear my prayer.

things on my heart:

_____
_____
_____
_____
_____
_____

highlights

_____
_____
_____
_____
_____
_____
_____

prayer requests

_____
_____
_____
_____
_____
_____

PSALM 118:5-6

When hard pressed,
I cried to the Lord;
he brought me into a
spacious place.
The Lord is with me;
I will not be afraid.
What can mere
mortals do to me?

REFLECT

FEAR

We will all experience pain at some point in our lives; it is inevitable. God desires a relationship with you that includes prayer and faith through both good times and bad. He is with you always and will never leave you.

Recall a painful time in your life. What happened? Did you find yourself relying on God to get you through it? How have you grown from that experience? What did you learn about yourself? How did your relationship with God change or grow?

_____

_____

_____

_____

_____

_____

_____

_____

_____

_____

_____

_____

_____

_____

_____

_____

_____

LORD, thank you

WEEK OF:

teach me

guide me

PSALM 102:17

He will respond to the prayer of the destitute;
he will not despise their plea.

things on my heart:

_____
_____
_____
_____
_____
_____

highlights

_____
_____
_____
_____
_____
_____

prayer requests

_____
_____
_____
_____
_____
_____

PROVERBS 31:30

Charm is
deceptive, and
beauty is fleeting;
but a woman
who fears the
Lord is to be
praised.

LOVE & INNER BEAUTY

The world is full of charming, beautiful things that will ultimately leave you empty and disappointed if you value them over God in your life. A woman who fears the Lord is to be praised, because she values God above everything else. He is the only one who can truly fulfill your deepest needs and desires, and the only one who won't leave you disappointed and empty in the long run! Believe in and accept God's sovereignty, and take refuge in Him, trusting in Him through the ebbs and flows of your life's journey.

What are some things that you find value in? Do these things carry the appropriate weight in your life, or do you overvalue them? Do you fear the Lord and trust God's sovereignty over your life?

teach me

guide me

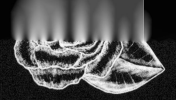

things on my heart:

_____
_____
_____
_____
_____
_____

_____
_____
_____
_____
_____
_____

_____
_____
_____
_____
_____
_____

ISAIAH 58:11

The Lord will
guide
you always; he will
satisfy
your needs in a
sun-scorched land and will
strengthen
your frame. You will be like a
well-watered garden, like a
spring whose waters never fail.

PROVISION & FAITHFULNESS

Have you ever felt unsure or ill-equipped to handle the unpredictable moments of life—issues with friends or loved ones, health concerns, the stress of a job, a loss, or even something you've battled within yourself? Know that God promises to guide you, to satisfy your needs, and will strengthen you to handle whatever life throws at you.

What are areas of your life (past or present) in which God has strengthened you and equipped you with all that you needed to handle life's curveballs?

_____

_____

_____

_____

_____

_____

_____

_____

_____

_____

_____

_____

_____

_____

_____

_____

_____

_____

_____

_____

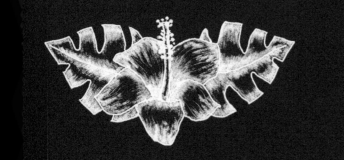

MATTHEW 7:11

If you, then, though you are evil, know how to give good gifts to your children, how much more will your Father in heaven give good gifts to those who ask him!

things on my heart:

_____
_____
_____
_____
_____
_____

highlights

_____
_____
_____
_____
_____
_____

prayer requests

_____
_____
_____
_____
_____
_____

JEREMIAH 29:13

You will seek me
and find me
when you
*seek me with
all your heart.*

REFLECT

GOD'S LOVE

Have you ever played a game of hide-and-seek? The "hider" hides and patiently waits until the seeker finishes their countdown and comes to find him or her. The seeker searches and searches until at last, the hider is found.

Fortunately, God doesn't work this way. He's not hiding from you, nor does He sit around in some hiding space waiting to reveal Himself if you are unable to find Him. He does, however, desire for you to seek Him. He's been right with you all along (whether you have been in communion with Him or not), with a desire for a loving connection! He wants you to seek Him! Pray to Him, open a dialogue with Him, and read His word. He has much to say to you and desires your heart!

Do you set aside time to be alone with God? What are ways that you seek the Lord? When do you feel closest to Him? What are some ways you feel He has spoken to you?

_____
_____
_____
_____
_____
_____
_____
_____
_____
_____
_____
_____
_____
_____
_____
_____

LORD, thank you

teach me

_____
_____
_____
_____
_____
_____
_____
_____
_____

guide me

_____
_____
_____
_____
_____
_____
_____
_____

_____
_____
_____
_____
_____
_____
_____
_____
_____
_____
_____
_____
_____
_____
_____
_____
_____
_____
_____
_____
_____
_____
_____
_____
_____
_____
_____

things on my heart:

_____
_____
_____
_____
_____
_____
_____

highlights

_____
_____
_____
_____
_____

prayer requests

_____
_____
_____
_____
_____
_____

MATTHEW 19:26

Jesus looked at them and said, "With man this is impossible, but *with God all things are possible.*"

Reflect

ADVERSITY & TRIALS

Repeat after me: "With God, all things are possible." Repeat it again. "With God ALL things are possible." If God said it, then you can be assured that it is absolutely true! If God can part seas, heal the blind, and bring men back from the dead, then you better believe He can certainly handle anything going on in your life!

Write about any areas of your life that feel uncertain. Are you working through any disappointments or facing a particular challenge? Perhaps you feel like you're in a good place, but you feel concern for someone else. Do you believe that God can handle all of the things on your heart?

_____

_____

_____

_____

_____

_____

_____

_____

_____

_____

_____

_____

_____

_____

_____

_____

_____

LORD, thank you

teach me

guide me

During the days of Jesus' life on earth, he offered up prayers and petitions with fervent cries and tears to the one who could save him from death, and he was heard because of his reverent submission.

things on my heart:

_____
_____
_____
_____
_____
_____

highlights

_____
_____
_____
_____
_____

prayer requests

_____
_____
_____
_____
_____

PSALM 37:4

Take delight in the Lord, and He will give you the desires of your heart.

REFLECT

AWE & SOVEREIGNTY

Everyone has hopes and desires for their lives. The desire to own a home, to have children and a family of your own, to be successful in your career, or to simply be healthy and happy are all good hopes and dreams to hold on to. However, know that to "take delight" in the Lord also means to trust Him and His perfect timing. You may want or desire something at this very moment in your life, but God may be telling you that it's not time yet. Maybe He wants to fulfill a desire you have in a completely different (and better) way than you imagine! There may be more He wants to accomplish through you, before fulfilling this dream or that. Perhaps He wants to use you to help fulfill someone else's dream or desire, or maybe the path He wants to take you along will lead you to one of your heart's desires. Keep the faith, delight in Him first, and trust that He loves you and knows what's best for you!

What are some of your heart's greatest desires? Do you share them with God? What are some hopes and desires the Lord has already fulfilled in your life?

_____

_____

_____

_____

_____

_____

_____

_____

_____

_____

_____

_____

LORD, thank you

teach me

_____
_____
_____
_____
_____
_____
_____
_____
_____
_____
_____
_____

guide me

_____
_____
_____
_____
_____
_____
_____
_____
_____

MARK 11:24

Therefore I tell you, whatever you ask for in prayer, believe
that you have received it, and it will be yours.

things on my heart:

_____
_____
_____
_____
_____
_____

_____
_____
_____
_____
_____
_____
_____

_____
_____
_____
_____
_____
_____
_____

ISAIAH 40:31

But those who hope in the Lord will renew their strength. They will soar on wings like eagles; they will run and not grow weary, they will walk and not be faint.

STRENGTH THROUGH FAITH

God desires that you trust Him, and He promises to give you strength.
Fully placing your trust in God may feel easier said than done, especially when circumstances seem difficult to handle, but His promises are good and true!

How do you handle your weaknesses and struggles? Do you take your feelings and concerns to God? Write about a time when God strengthened you to handle something that seemed impossible to you at the time.

LORD, thank you

teach me

guide me

LUKE 18:1

Then Jesus told his disciples a parable to show them that
they should always pray and not give up.

things on my heart:

_____

_____

_____

_____

_____

_____

highlights

prayer requests

_____

_____

_____

_____

_____

_____

_____

_____

HEBREWS 4:16

Let us then approach God's throne of grace with confidence, so that we may

receive mercy and find grace

to help us in our time of need.

GRACE & FORGIVENESS

Have you ever pondered the amazing grace and mercy that God grants us through His son Jesus Christ? As sinners, we deserved death and permanent separation from God as our ultimate punishment. However, God's love for us is so great, so unmeasurable, that He sent His one and only Son, Jesus Christ, to die on the cross so that if we accept and believe in Him, we are saved from eternal punishment! The God and creator of this universe loves YOU so much that He was willing to sacrifice His son as an offering so that He could have a relationship with YOU. How amazing is that!?

Do you ever struggle to accept God's love and grace, in spite of things you've done in your past? Share your thoughts below.

_____
_____
_____
_____
_____
_____
_____
_____
_____
_____
_____
_____
_____
_____
_____
_____
_____
_____

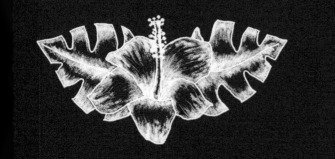

guide me

1 JOHN 1:9

If we confess our sins, he is faithful and just and will forgive us our sins and purify us from all unrighteousness.

things on my heart:

_____
_____
_____
_____
_____
_____

highlights

prayer requests

_____
_____
_____
_____
_____
_____

_____
_____
_____
_____
_____
_____
_____

1 JOHN 3:18

Dear children, let us not *love* with words or speech but *with actions and in truth.*

REFLECT

LOVE & INNER BEAUTY

"Actions speak louder than words." This ever-popular phrase is used to show that words can be meaningless if they're not demonstrated through action. Think of someone who says that they want to get in shape but continues to eat unhealthy food and avoid exercise. Certainly, this person's actions speak louder than their words.

The same idea holds with love. Words can be meaningful, but action proves those words are true! Love is shown through action. A husband who takes care of his sick wife, a neighbor who bakes a batch of your favorite muffins for no reason, or a co-worker who helps you finish a project they won't receive any recognition from—these are all examples of ways to demonstrate love through action!

What are ways that you can love others through your actions? What are some of the uniquely God-given talents and abilities that YOU can use to show others your love? Conversely, what actions from others make you feel the most loved?

_____

_____

_____

_____

_____

_____

_____

_____

_____

_____

_____

_____

PSALM 141:2

May my prayer be set before you like incense; may the lifting
up of my hands be like the evening sacrifice.

things on my heart:

highlights

prayer requests

1 CORINTHIANS 10:13

No temptation has overtaken
you except what is common
to mankind. And

God is faithful;

he will not let you be tempted
beyond what you can bear.
But when you are tempted,

*he will also
provide a way out*

so that you can endure it.

PROVISION & FAITHFULNESS

The first sin paved the way for the sins that are prevalent in today's world. The urge to submit to worldly temptations or to indulge in the notion of "the grass is greener on the other side" is all too common, especially when things get hard.

God promises to protect you from ever being tempted beyond your ability to resist, and to help you to endure those temptations. Be encouraged that whatever temptations exist around you, or whatever temptation you are fighting, God is faithful! He promises to provide a path out! Open your heart to Him and seek His promises. He's there, even when you feel overwhelmed by temptation.

What temptations do you struggle with? Do you seek God and His support when you feel overwhelmingly tempted? Reflect on a time when God provided a way out of a tempting situation.

LORD, thank you

teach me

_____
_____
_____
_____
_____
_____
_____
_____
_____
_____
_____

guide me

_____
_____
_____
_____
_____
_____
_____
_____
_____
_____

MATTHEW 26:41

Watch and pray so that you will not fall into temptation. The spirit is willing, but the flesh is weak.

things on my heart:

_____
_____
_____
_____
_____
_____
_____

highlights

_____
_____
_____
_____
_____
_____

prayer requests

_____
_____
_____
_____
_____
_____

ROMANS 8:28

And we know
that in all things
*God works for the
good of those who
love him,*
who have been
called according
to his purpose.

REFLECT

ADVERSITY & TRIALS

Just like the story of Joseph, and the trials he went through that ultimately led to him saving his own people in Egypt, God can also use the trials and circumstances in your life for good! There is nothing you will endure that hasn't first gone through God and His authority. Recall that in the midst of his suffering, Joseph had no idea that God was using these events in his life to orchestrate a plan to save his people through him!

Trust that God loves you, that He knows what is best for you, and that He has a plan for your future. He is working the events of your life out for your good, even when you can't see His work in the midst of it. Keep the faith!

Reflect on a trial or challenge you have experienced in your life that ultimately resulted in something positive. Did you trust God during that time? Was your faith ultimately strengthened as a result of walking with God through this challenge? Are you in the midst of a trial or suffering now? If so, consider how God might be trying to work through and with you in the midst of this challenging time.

LORD, thank you

teach me

guide me

MATTHEW 21:22

If you believe, you will receive
whatever you ask for in prayer.

things on my heart:

_____

_____

_____

_____

_____

_____

_____

highlights

_____

_____

_____

_____

_____

prayer requests

_____

_____

_____

_____

_____

LAMENTATIONS 3:22-23

Because of the Lord's great love we are not consumed, for *his compassions never fail.* They are new every morning; *great is your faithfulness.*

GOD'S LOVE

You are loved and cherished by the creator of the universe. He has special plans for your life and is full of compassion and mercy for you! As human beings, we are all imperfect and susceptible to our sinful natures. However, God's love and mercy for His children are endless, no matter what. Each new morning is symbolic as the light breaks through the darkness. In the same way, your fellowship with Christ can overcome any sin, guilt, or hardship in your life!

Do you trust that God loves you and has never-ending compassion for you—past, present, and future? Use this space to write about any areas of your life where you struggle and would benefit from being more open to God's love and compassion.

LORD, thank you

teach me

guide me

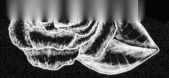

Very early in the morning, while it was still dark, Jesus got up, left the house and went off to a solitary place, where he prayed.

things on my heart:

_____
_____
_____
_____
_____
_____

highlights

prayer requests

_____
_____
_____
_____
_____
_____
_____

_____
_____
_____
_____
_____
_____
_____

PROVERBS 3:5

Trust in the Lord with *all your heart* and lean not on your own understanding.

AWE & SOVEREIGNTY

As humans, we may struggle to fully comprehend all that happens in our lives and in the world around us. You might feel frustrated at the outcome of a particular situation or find that the plans you had for your life have gone a completely different direction. Even so, God wants you to trust Him! He is sovereign! Be encouraged, knowing that the creator of the entire universe loves you and knows what's best for you.

Write about a situation that required you to really trust in the Lord. What happened? Did this experience strengthen your faith? What was the outcome?

_____
_____
_____
_____
_____
_____
_____
_____
_____
_____
_____
_____
_____
_____
_____
_____
_____
_____
_____
_____
_____

LORD, thank you

teach me

guide me

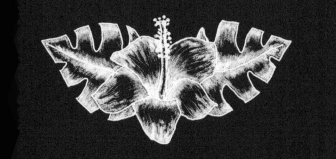

things on my heart:

_____
_____
_____
_____
_____
_____

_____
_____
_____
_____
_____
_____

_____
_____
_____
_____
_____

PROVERBS 31:25

She is clothed
with *strength*
and *dignity*;
she can laugh at
the days
to come.

REFLECT

STRENGTH THROUGH FAITH

As women, we wear a lot of hats. We are moms, wives, daughters, students, teachers, chefs, taxi drivers, busy professionals—and often we fill many of these roles (or all of them!) at the same time! It can be overwhelming, but you can have confidence knowing that God has equipped you to handle all of life's roles, no matter the difficulty. God promises to strengthen you and never leave you.

Write about a time when you were faced with a challenge, adversity, or the unknown, but felt a sense of peace and confidence regardless. Did you go to God during this time? Did you feel His strength?

_____

_____

_____

_____

_____

_____

_____

_____

_____

_____

_____

_____

_____

_____

_____

_____

_____

LORD, thank you

teach me

guide me

EPHESIANS 6:18

And pray in the Spirit on all occasions and with all kinds of prayers and requests. With this in mind, be alert and always keep on praying for all the Lord's people.

things on my heart:

highlights

prayer requests

MATTHEW 6:34

Therefore *do not worry about tomorrow,* for tomorrow will worry about itself. Each day has enough trouble of its own.

FEAR

It can be difficult to remain "in the moment" and to live each day as it comes. Are you a worrier? Do you fret over endless to-do lists, or over things that are beyond your control? What joys and struggles are relevant to you this very day? What techniques can you use to focus on the present moment, knowing that you are exactly where God knew you would be at this time in your life?

JOHN 16:23-24

In that day, you will no longer ask me anything. Very truly I tell you, my Father will give you whatever you ask in my name. Until now you have not asked for anything in my name. Ask and you will receive, and your joy will be complete.

things on my heart:

highlights

prayer requests

EPHESIANS 4:2

Be completely *humble* and *gentle;* be *patient,* bearing with one another in *love.*

REFLECT

LOVE & INNER BEAUTY

God desires our hearts to be humble, gentle, patient, and full of love for one another. In a dog-eat-dog world where "instant gratification" has become the norm, these qualities can so easily become lost.

What are some ways that you can demonstrate a heart that is humble, gentle, patient, and loving to those around you, from casual acquaintances to your most cherished loved ones, and everyone in-between? Do you struggle with any of these traits? What are some ways that others display these qualities to you?

LORD, thank you

teach me

_____
_____
_____
_____
_____
_____
_____
_____
_____
_____
_____

guide me

_____
_____
_____
_____
_____
_____
_____
_____

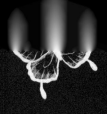

things on my heart:

_____
_____
_____
_____
_____
_____

highlights

_____
_____
_____
_____
_____
_____

prayer requests

_____
_____
_____
_____
_____
_____

PROVERBS 27:9

Perfume and
incense bring
joy to the heart,
and the pleasantness
of a friend springs
from their heartfelt
advice.

PROVISION & FAITHFULNESS

The phrase "Friends become our chosen family" is a popular saying. Friends, like family, bring comfort, honesty, and love (and sometimes challenges) to our lives. They are the people we can be silly with, cry with, laugh with, and tell our deepest thoughts to.

Whatever season of life you are in, know that God knows and is with you. God knew who would be closest to you at this time in your life! Think about this: the world is home to over seven billion people. With that many people, you are only acquainted with a relatively small number. Even smaller is the number of people whom you are close to, and smaller still are the people who know you fully.
This is not by accident!

Who are some of your closest friends? What makes them so special to you?
How are you a good friend to them?

LORD, thank you

teach me

guide me

MATTHEW 18:20

For where two or three gather in my name,
there am I with them.

things on my heart:

_____
_____
_____
_____
_____
_____

highlights

_____
_____
_____
_____
_____

prayer requests

_____
_____
_____
_____
_____

2 CORINTHIANS 9:8

And God is able to bless you abundantly, so that in all things at all times, having all that you need, you will abound in every good work.

AWE & SOVEREIGNTY

The Bible is full of countless examples of people—average people, just like you and I—whom God chose to do big things for His kingdom. Think of Moses leading the Israelites out of Egypt, Esther risking her life for her people, and Jonah warning the people of Nineveh, among others. Through Scripture, we know that many of these people doubted themselves and felt unqualified to do what they were asked to do—even to the point of pleading with God to choose someone else!

Have you ever felt called to do something, but also felt unsure of yourself, and how in the world God could use you to accomplish it? Even now, do you have an opportunity before you that both scares and excites you, all at the same time? Write about an experience like this. Always remember that God will guide you. If He is calling you, He alone will qualify YOU and grant you the grace to rise to the challenge!

teach me

guide me

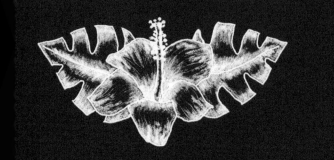

And when you pray, do not keep on babbling like pagans, for they think they will be heard because of their many words. Do not be like them, for your Father knows what you need before you ask him.

things on my heart

_____
_____
_____
_____
_____
_____
_____

highlights

_____
_____
_____
_____
_____
_____
_____

prayer requests

_____
_____
_____
_____
_____
_____

PSALM 46:10

He says,
*"Be still and know
that I am God.*
I will be exalted
among the nations,
I will be exalted
in the earth."

REFLECT

STRENGTH THROUGH FAITH

Life can be hectic. There are endless to-do lists: places to go, people to see, and work to be done. Daily life can be overwhelming, especially if you are dealing with more significant trials at the same time. God promises that He will be with you in any and every situation you are faced with.

Sometimes, we get so wrapped up in our own lives that we forget to sit back and remember who God is. You may think that you need to have it all figured out, and that you need to constantly be in the driver's seat—but you don't. He instructs us to be still. Let Him be God! Let HIM be YOUR helper! It's that quiet, still space where God can enter in and speak to your heart, giving you peace and rest at the same time. Let Him handle your battles— give them to Him! Share your heart with Him and let Him work.

Do you find it difficult to be still at times? Do you feel like you have to accomplish all the pressures of your day-to-day schedule? What are some ways that you can be still and let God step in for you?

_____

_____

_____

_____

_____

_____

_____

_____

_____

_____

_____

_____

_____

things on my heart:

highlights

prayer requests

2 CORINTHIANS 12:9

But he said to me,
"My grace is sufficient for you, for my power is made perfect in weakness." Therefore I will boast all the more gladly about my weaknesses, so that Christ's power may rest upon me.

GRACE & FORGIVENESS

Life can feel overwhelming and hard. There are things to do, families to feed, activities to attend, money to make, and in between all of those things, unexpected moments often arise.

Trust that even during your most difficult times, the Lord is near! He is all the grace you need each and every day, especially for the things that didn't get done, the mistakes you made, and the daily hardships you face. HIS power is perfected in your weakest moments. It's in the acknowledgment that you can't do it all, that you are in fact human, that God steps in and says, "I'm all you need. Share your heart with me. Let me give you rest."

What things in your life do you find overwhelming at times? Do you go to God in your weakest moments, seeking His strength and grace? Share about a time that you felt overwhelmed and had the opportunity to experience God's grace.

_____
_____
_____
_____
_____
_____
_____
_____
_____
_____
_____
_____
_____
_____
_____
_____
_____
_____

teach me

_____
_____
_____
_____
_____
_____
_____
_____
_____
_____

guide me

_____
_____
_____
_____
_____
_____
_____
_____

1 PETER 3:12

For the eyes of the Lord are on the righteous and his ears are attentive to their prayer, but the face of the Lord is against those who do evil.

things on my heart:

_____

_____

_____

_____

_____

_____

highlights

_____

_____

_____

_____

_____

_____

prayer requests

_____

_____

_____

_____

_____

_____

ROMANS 12:9

Love must be sincere. Hate what is evil; *cling to what is good.*

REFLECT

LOVE & INNER BEAUTY

To be sincere means that you have genuine feelings about or for something, free of pretense or deceit. Have you ever done something with the wrong motive? Perhaps you were doing something kind because you wanted recognition, or maybe you were doing something loving for someone because you were told to do so, not because you wanted to. God calls us to love sincerely and to cling to what is good!

What are ways that you love the people around you—your colleagues, acquaintances, family, and friends? On the other hand, how do they treat you with love? What actions make you feel the most loved?

_____
_____
_____
_____
_____
_____
_____
_____
_____
_____
_____
_____
_____
_____
_____
_____
_____
_____

LORD, thank you

teach me

guide me

1 TIMOTHY 2:8

Therefore I want the men everywhere to pray, lifting up holy hands without anger or disputing.

things on my heart:

_____
_____
_____
_____
_____
_____

highlights

_____
_____
_____
_____
_____
_____

prayer requests

_____
_____
_____
_____
_____
_____

ISAIAH 30:21

Whether you turn to the right or to the left, your ears will hear a voice behind you, saying, *"This is the way; walk in it."*

PROVISION & FAITHFULNESS

Throughout Scripture, we read how God spoke to countless people, directing their paths and guiding them in the way they should go. While the way God speaks to you today may be a little different (not quite so audible), He nevertheless still communicates with you and leads you in the way He desires! This requires you to be still, to listen, to engage with Him in prayer, and to recognize how you feel. Listen for that still, small voice. That gentle whisper from Him. If you align with Him and His word and feel peace about a decision, trust that it is the right one!

Have you ever found yourself faced with choices and feeling unsure of the right path? Maybe it was a job change, a decision to move somewhere else, a financial decision, a health choice, or even a change in your relationship. How did you make a final decision about what to do? Do you go to God when you feel unsure? Have you ever felt Him directing your steps?

LORD, thank you

WEEK OF:

teach me

guide me

JOHN 15:7

If you remain in me and my words remain in you, ask
whatever you wish, and it will be done for you.

things on my heart:

_____
_____
_____
_____
_____
_____

highlights

_____
_____
_____
_____
_____

prayer requests

_____
_____
_____
_____
_____
_____

215

PROVERBS 17:17

A friend loves at all times, and a brother is born for a time of adversity.

You were created for relationships. God himself wants and desires your heart and for you to be in a loving relationship with Him. He knew you would be exactly where you are today, among the people you're surrounded by, the friends you have, and the family you were born into. These are the people that you can connect with, relate to, share burdens and joys with, and love in the way that God desires.

What makes someone a good friend? Share about a time that a friend or family member had a real impact on you. How did they make you feel? What did they do? What are some ways that you can love those around you?

LORD, thank you

teach me

guide me

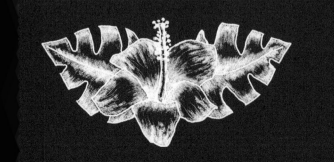

MARK 11:25

And when you stand praying, if you hold anything against anyone, forgive them, so that your Father in heaven may forgive you your sins.

things on my heart:

_____
_____
_____
_____
_____
_____
_____

highlights

_____
_____
_____
_____
_____
_____
_____

prayer requests

_____
_____
_____
_____
_____
_____
_____

MATTHEW 6:26-27

Look at the birds of the air;
they do not sow or reap or
store away in barns, and
yet your heavenly Father
feeds them.

*Are you not much
more valuable
than they?*

Can any one of you by
worrying add a single
hour to your life?

REFLECT

FEAR

The demands of life can be stressful. The financial obligations, parental responsibilities, health concerns, and career duties can all cause pressure in our day-to-day lives. God reminds us how valuable we are to Him, and how much He cares for you and your needs. If he can fulfill the daily needs of the birds and creatures of the earth, then He will certainly fulfill yours!

Do you place your cares and worries, hopes and joys at God's feet, and believe that God will always meet your needs? What things in your life bring you joy? What areas of your life do you worry about?

_____

_____

_____

_____

_____

_____

_____

_____

_____

_____

_____

_____

_____

_____

_____

_____

_____

WEEK OF:

teach me

guide me

PSALM 55:17

Evening, morning and noon I cry out in distress, and he hears my voice.

things on my heart:

_____
_____
_____
_____
_____
_____

highlights

_____
_____
_____
_____
_____
_____

prayer requests

_____
_____
_____
_____
_____
_____
_____

Answered Prayers:

PRAYER REQUEST	PRAYER DATE	DATE ANSWERED

Answered Prayers

PRAYER REQUEST	PRAYER DATE	DATE ANSWERED

Answered Prayers:

PRAYER REQUEST	PRAYER DATE	DATE ANSWERED

Answered ♡ Prayers:

PRAYER REQUEST	PRAYER DATE	DATE ANSWERED

Answered Prayers:

PRAYER REQUEST	PRAYER DATE	DATE ANSWERED
_____	_____	_____
_____	_____	_____
_____	_____	_____
_____	_____	_____
_____	_____	_____
_____	_____	_____
_____	_____	_____
_____	_____	_____
_____	_____	_____
_____	_____	_____
_____	_____	_____
_____	_____	_____
_____	_____	_____
_____	_____	_____
_____	_____	_____
_____	_____	_____
_____	_____	_____
_____	_____	_____
_____	_____	_____
_____	_____	_____
_____	_____	_____
_____	_____	_____
_____	_____	_____

Answered Prayers

PRAYER REQUEST	PRAYER DATE	DATE ANSWERED

About the Author

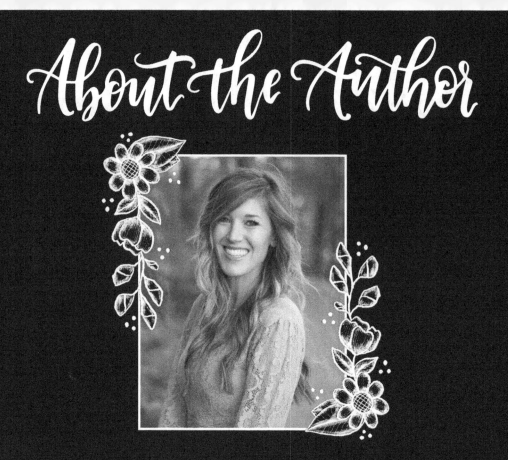

Shannon is a wife and mother with a heart for Jesus. After becoming a stay-at-home mom from her teaching career in 2011, she stepped out in faith and in 2014 started a small business selling her art creations in an Etsy® shop called *The White Lime*. There, she sells prints and cards of her hand-drawn chalk art and watercolor designs, all of which center around her life experiences and faith in God. Her work has also been sold globally, and in stores across the country through the companies and manufacturers she partners with. An Instagram® design she posted of one of her chalk art pieces back in 2016 paved the way for her partnership with Paige Tate & Co., and since then, the two have partnered together on several publications.

Shannon loves spending time with her family, and also has a passion for health and fitness. She makes time to work out and clear her mind several times per week. Her faith is incredibly important to her, and each unimaginable door that God opens serves as confirmation that He is walking this journey with her. Shannon resides with her husband and two children in Maryland. To learn more about Shannon and her work, you can visit her website www.thewhitelime.etsy.com or her Instagram® page @shannonroberts19, where she posts behind-the-scenes images and upcoming projects.

 @shannonroberts19

MORE FROM SHANNON ROBERTS

Find on Amazon, Barnes & Noble and wherever books are sold!

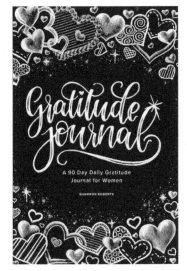

Gratitude Journal

A 90 Day Daily Gratitude Journal for Women

Chalk Art & Lettering 101

An Intro to Chalkboard Lettering, Illustration, Design, and more

Life is Sweet

A Chalkboard Coloring Book

Chalk it up to Grace

A Chalkboard Coloring Book with Removable Wall Art Prints

Made in the USA
Coppell, TX
17 October 2020